Scott Foresman   Gr

Math Around the Clock

SUMMER SCHOOL • AFTER SCHOOL • INTERSESSION

Place Value, Addition, and Subtraction of Whole Numbers

PEARSON

Scott Foresman

Editorial Offices:
Glenview, Illinois • Parsippany, New Jersey • New York, New York

Sales Offices:
Parsippany, New Jersey • Duluth, Georgia • Glenview, Illinois
Coppell, Texas • Ontario, California • Mesa, Arizona

ISBN: 0-328-06366-5

Copyright © 2003 Pearson Education, Inc.

2 3 4 5 6 7 8 9 10 V004 12 11 10 09 08 07 06 05 04 03

Math Around the Clock

Contents

How many groups of 1 million do you need to make 1 billion? How many groups of 10 million do you need to make 1 billion?

Place Value Through Millions

Example 1

Write 705,637,023 in word form and in short word form.

Word form: seven hundred five million, six hundred thirty-seven thousand, twenty-three in standard form; Short word form: 705 million, 637 thousand, 23

Example 2

Write the value of the underlined digit in 3<u>6</u>,925,048. The underlined digit is in the millions place, so the value of the underlined digit is 6,000,000.

Example 3

Write 21,304,201 in expanded form.
Expanded form: 20,000,000 + 1,000,000 + 300,000 + 4,000 + 200 + 1

Write each number in word form and in short word form.

1 2,160,500 _____

_____

_____

2 91,207,040 _____

_____

_____

3 510,200,450 _____

_____

_____

Place Value Through Millions (continued)

Write the value of the underlined digit.

4 4,5_6_2,398   **5** 1_5_,347,025   **6** 37,81_4_,956

_____   _____   _____

7 _5_26,878,953   **8** 782,354,0_6_5   **9** 9_1_8,403,760

_____   _____   _____

10 An underground rail system in Osaka, Japan, carries 988,600,000 passengers per year. Write this number in expanded form.

_____

11 **Algebra** What missing number would make the number sentence 3,589,000 = 3,000,000 + ■ + 80,000 + 9,000 true?

_____

12 **Math Reasoning** What number can be added to 999,990 to make 1,000,000?

_____

13 **Test Prep** Choose the correct letter for each answer.

Which of the following gives the value of the underlined digit in the number 5_2_,685,941?

A 5,000,000   **B** 50,000   **C** 500,000   **D** 50,000,000   **E** NH

14 The United States has about 147,200,000 car owners. Which of the following shows this number in expanded form?

F 100,000 + 40,000 + 7,000 + 200

G 100,000,000 + 40,000,000 + 7,000,000 + 200,000

H 100,000,000 + 40,000,000 + 7,000 + 200

J 10,000,000 + 4,000,000 + 700,000 + 200

Source: Factastic Book of 1001 Lists, 1999.

Name _____

Place Value Through Millions

1 Which shows this number in standard form?

80,000,000 + 700,000 + 50,000 + 6,000 + 500 + 3

- **A** 87,056,503
- **B** 80,756,503
- **C** 8,756,503
- **D** 8,750,653

2 Which is the word name for 8,700,012?

- **F** Eight thousand, seven hundred twelve
- **G** Eight million, seven hundred twelve
- **H** Eight million, seventy thousand, twelve
- **J** Eight million, seven hundred thousand, twelve

3 Which is the standard form for the number six million, four hundred fifty thousand, eighty-six?

- **A** 6,450,860
- **B** 6,450,086
- **C** 6,045,086
- **D** 6,450,806

4 What is the value of the 7 in 73,845,302?

- **F** Seventy
- **G** Seventy thousand
- **H** Seven million
- **J** Seventy million

5 What is the name for this number?

4,700,050

- **A** Forty-seven thousand, fifty
- **B** Forty-seven million, fifty
- **C** Four million, seventy thousand, fifty
- **D** Four million, seven hundred thousand, fifty

6 What is the value of the 4 in 224,759,600?

- **F** Four thousand
- **G** Forty thousand
- **H** Four hundred thousand
- **J** Four million

7 The planet closest to the sun is Mercury. It is about 36,000,000 miles from the sun. What is this distance in short word form?

- **A** 3 billion 6 million
- **B** 36 thousand
- **C** 36 million
- **D** 36 billion

8 What is the value of the digit 6 in the number 526,332,871?

- **F** 6 billion
- **G** 600 thousand
- **H** 6 hundred thousand
- **J** 6 million

Oral Directions Choose the correct letter for each answer.

Place Value Through Billions

Example 1

Find the value of the underlined digit in 63<u>7</u>,847,295,000.
The 7 is in the billions place.
The value of the underlined 7 in 63<u>7</u>,847,295,000 is 7,000,000,000.

Example 2

Write 637,847,295,000 in expanded form. Find the value of each digit according to its place. Then express 637,847,295,000 as the sum of the value of its digits.

The expanded form of 637,847,295,000 is 600,000,000,000 + 30,000,000,000 + 7,000,000,000 + 800,000,000 + 40,000,000 + 7,000,000 + 200,000 + 90,000 + 5,000.

Write the value of each underlined digit.

1 <u>3</u>4,906,483,201

_____

2 <u>6</u>43,514,008,311

_____

3 909,<u>0</u>08,446,000

_____

4 <u>7</u>,000,574,300

_____

5 1<u>0</u>9,321,600,004

_____

6 <u>5</u>76,333,741,612

_____

7 Write 13,497,808,070 in expanded form.

_____

_____

_____

8 Write 684,713,004,364 in expanded form.

_____

_____

Place Value Through Billions (continued)

Write the value of the underlined digit.

9 6̲5,907,007,250

_____

10 1̲60,379,450,000

_____

11 43̲,614,490,712

_____

12 6̲0,897,470,000

_____

13 The 1999 estimated population of India was 1,000,848,550. What digit is in the billions place? _____

Use the table at the right for Exercises 14–17.

World Population Estimates	
1960	3,039,332,401
1970	3,707,610,112
1980	4,456,705,217
1990	5,283,757,267
2000	6,823,766,067

14 Find the 1970 population estimate. What is the value of the three? _____

15 Write the 2000 population estimate in expanded form.

_____

_____

16 How many billions lived on Earth in 1990? _____

17 How many more billions lived on Earth in 1990 than in 1960? _____

18 The 1999 estimated population for China was 1,246,871,900. Write this in expanded form.

_____

_____

19 **Test Prep** Choose the correct letter for each answer.

What digit is in the ten billions place in the number six hundred fifty-three billion, nine hundred million?

A 6   **B** 3   **C** 9   **D** 5

20 What is the value of the underlined digit? 314̲,478,494,016

F 4,000,000,000   **G** 400,000,000   **H** 4,000   **J** 40,000,000,000

Place Value Through Billions

1 Tyrone read that the profits of a toy company were $12 billion last year. Which of the following shows this number in standard form?

A $12,000

B $12,000,000

C $12,000,000,000

D $1,200,000,000,000

2 Which is the value of the underlined digit in 45,813,009,004?

F 5 hundred thousand

G 50 million

H 5 hundred million

J 5 billion

3 Which shows the number two billion, sixteen million, seven thousand written in standard form?

A 2,160,007

B 2,106,000,007

C 2,160,000,007

D 2,016,007,000

4 Which is the value of the 6 in 2,378,604,117?

F 6,000,000

G 600,000

H 60,000

J 6,000

Oral Directions Choose the correct letter for each answer.

© Scott Foresman

Place Value Through Billions (continued)

5 Which is the expanded form for nine billion, six hundred thousand, fifty?

   A 9,000,000,000 + 600,000 + 50

   B 9,000,000,000 + 60,000 + 50

   C 9,000,000,000 + 650,000

   D 9,000,000 + 600,000 + 50

6 Which shows the number five billion, five million, five thousand, fifty written in standard form?

   F 5,050,050,050

   G 5,005,005,050

   H 5,005,050,050

   J 5,050,005,005

7 Which is the value of the 3 in 639,204,986,241?

   A Thirty

   B Thirty thousand

   C Thirty million

   D Thirty billion

8 Which is the value of the 8 in 87,365,002,394?

   F 80,000,000,000

   G 80,000,000

   H 80,000

   J 8,000

What is the greatest 5-digit number that can be written using each odd digit only once?

What is the least 5-digit number that can be written using each odd digit only once?

Name _____

Example

Compare 15,685,200 and 15,676,200.

Step 1 Line up the numbers to compare the digits.

15,6 8 5,200
15,6 7 6,200

↑ same   ↑ different

The ten thousands digits are different.

Step 2 Compare the ten thousands.

8 is more than 7, so 15,685,200 is more than 15,676,200.

You can write 15,685,200 > 15,676,200 or 15,676,200 < 15,685,200.

Compare. Use > or < for each ●.

1 365,485 ● 343,900

2 5,681,400 ● 5,980,100

3 7,410,910 ● 7,412,000

4 12,085,900 ● 12,079,900

5 29,000,700 ● 29,000,701

6 243,150,000 ● 243,740,000

7 918,456,661 ● 918,423,701

8 405,744,581 ● 405,744,568

Order the numbers from greatest to least.

9 518,681; 51,995; 5,094,156; 5,814

_____

10 8,205,319; 8,371,000; 80,570,000; 8,201,415

_____

11 21,879,400; 218,794,000; 21,870,500; 2,999,900

_____

12 975,041,700; 970,590,800; 97,900,599; 985,000,000

_____

Comparing and Ordering Numbers (continued)

Compare. Use > or < for each ●.

13 1,689,000 ● 1,679,000

_____

14 43,914,500 ● 43,925,000

_____

15 62,441,300 ● 62,329,500

_____

16 518,495,000 ● 517,954,000

_____

Order the numbers from greatest to least.

17 96,500; 8,400,509; 8,946,000; 81,000,900

_____

18 746,589,415; 497,956,881; 749,300,000; 719,995,800

_____

Use the table at the right for Exercises 19–21.

19 Which country is largest in population?

_____

20 Which country is least populated?

_____

21 Which country has the greater population, Peru or Venezuela? _____

Populations	
Argentina	36,202,000
Bolivia	7,680,000
Brazil	169,545,000
Chile	14,996,000
Colombia	39,172,000
Peru	26,198,000
Venezuela	23,596,000

Source: Factastic Book of 1001 Lists.

22 **Test Prep** Choose the correct letter for each answer.

Which number is greatest?

A 59,814,000 **B** 59,819,000 **C** 5,999,900 **D** 500,000,000 **E** NH

23 Which of these four countries has the smallest area? Brazil, 3,286,472 square miles; Canada, 3,851,788 square miles; China, 3,704,426 square miles; United States, 3,617,827 square miles

F Brazil **G** Canada **H** China **J** United States **K** NH

Name _____

1 Which list shows these numbers ordered from greatest to least?

50,500; 55,505; 55,000; 50,000

- **A** 50,000; 55,000; 50,500; 55,505
- **B** 50,000; 50,500; 55,000; 55,505
- **C** 55,505; 50,000; 50,500; 55,000
- **D** 55,505; 55,000; 50,500; 50,000

2 The table shows the weights of several aircraft. Which list shows the weights from least to greatest?

Weights of World's Aircraft	
B121 Monoplane	1,600 lb
Boeing 747	775,000 lb
Boeing B-52H	488,000 lb
Saturn V Rocket	6,526,000 lb
Wright Brothers plane	750 lb

- **F** 750; 1,600; 488,000; 775,000; 6,526,000
- **G** 1,600; 750; 488,000; 775,000; 6,526,000
- **H** 1,600; 488,000; 6,526,000; 750; 750,000
- **J** 6,526,000; 775,000; 488,000; 1,600; 750

3 Compare. Choose the correct symbol.

16,398,263,056 ● 16,388,263,058

- **A** +
- **B** >
- **C** <
- **D** =

4 Which list shows these numbers ordered from greatest to least?

- **F** 7,890,900; 7,809,900; 5,475,700; 4,979,450
- **G** 7,809,900; 7,890,900; 5,475,700; 4,979,450
- **H** 4,979,450; 5,475,700; 7,890,900; 7,809,900
- **J** 4,979,450; 5,475,700; 7,809,900; 7,890,900

5 Which choice makes the statement true?

465,980 > ■

- **A** 465,990
- **B** Four hundred thousand, nine hundred ninety
- **C** Four million, nine hundred
- **D** 4,650,980

Oral Directions Choose the correct letter for each answer.

A number has 2 in its ones place. Its tenths value is twice that number. It has a zero in the hundredths place. Its thousandths digit is the sum of the ones and tenths digit. What is the number?

Place Value Through Thousandths

Example 1

Find the value of the 7 in 3.872.

ones	tenths	hundredths	thousandths
3	8	7	2

The 7 is in the hundredths place. Its value is 0.07, which is read "seven hundredths."

Example 2

Write 5.694 using words.

ones	tenths	hundredths	thousandths
5	6	9	4

It is written five and six hundred ninety-four thousandths.

Write the value of each underlined digit.

1 61.5<u>3</u>8   **2** 379.01<u>7</u>   **3** 2.5<u>5</u>3   **4** 0.38<u>1</u>

_____   _____   _____   _____

5 6.<u>6</u>47   **6** 300.1<u>3</u>5   **7** 14.70<u>4</u>   **8** 819.00<u>3</u>

_____   _____   _____   _____

9 57.9<u>8</u>1   **10** 701.08<u>6</u>   **11** 0.<u>5</u>47   **12** 9.0<u>9</u>7

_____   _____   _____   _____

13 Write 2.598 in word form.

_____

_____

14 Write 37.207 in word form.

_____

_____

Place Value Through Thousandths (continued)

Write the value of the underlined digit.

15 77.01<u>7</u>   **16** 432.<u>8</u>19   **17** 6.1<u>5</u>4   **18** 12.8<u>1</u>6

_____   _____   _____   _____

19 586.0<u>2</u>   **20** 7.34<u>9</u>   **21** 0.<u>8</u>   **22** 63.0<u>7</u>6

_____   _____   _____   _____

Write each number in standard form.

23 19 and 62 hundredths   **24** 507 thousandths   **25** 4 and 2 tenths

_____   _____   _____

Use the table at the right for Exercises 26–28.

26 Write Jenny's 1997 batting average using words.

_____

_____

Jenny's Batting Averages	
1996	0.392
1997	0.418
1998	0.407
1999	0.496
2000	0.491

27 **Math Reasoning** In place value terms, why was 1999 a better year for Jenny's batting average than 2000? Explain.

_____

28 Which year did Jenny have a batting average of four hundred seven thousandths?   _____

29 **Test Prep** Choose the correct letter for each answer.

How many hundredths are in 581.273?

A 5   **B** 1   **C** 7   **D** 2

30 Which number sentence is true?

F 0.8 > 0.9   **G** 3.07 < 3.7   **H** 8.0 < 0.8   **J** 0.08 = 0.80

Name _____

1 Which is the place value of the 5 in 421.365?

  A Thousandths

  B Hundredths

  C Tenths

  D Thousands

2 Which is three and thirty-one thousandths in decimal form?

  F 331,000   **H** 3.301

  G 3.3100   **J** 3.031

3 Write 4.043 in word form.

  A Four and forty-three hundredths

  B Forty and forty-three hundredths

  C Forty and forty-three thousandths

  D Four and forty-three thousandths

4 Which digit in this number is in the thousandths place? 84.625

  F 2   **H** 5

  G 4   **J** 6

5 Which is four hundred twelve thousandths in decimal form?

  A 0.412   **C** 4.012

  B 4.12   **D** 400.012

6 What is the value of the 4 in 0.347?

  F Four tenths

  G Four hundredths

  H Four thousandths

  J Four

7 Which is eight thousandths in decimal form?

  A 8.000   **C** 0.080

  B 0.800   **D** 0.008

8 What is the value of the 6 in 321.609?

  F Six tenths

  G Six hundredths

  H Six thousandths

  J Six

9 Write 11.32 in word form.

  A Eleven and thirty-two

  B Eleven and thirty-two tenths

  C Eleven and thirty-two hundredths

  D Eleven and thirty-two thousandths

10 Which digit is in the hundredths place? 698.524

  F 2   **H** 5

  G 4   **J** 6

Oral Directions Choose the correct letter for each answer.

© Scott Foresman

Is ⁻8°C colder or warmer than ⁻15°C?

Justify your answer using a number line.

Name _____

Example 1

Compare ⁻1 and ⁻5.

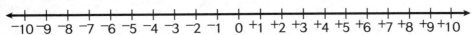

On the number line, ⁻5 is to the left of ⁻1, so ⁻5 is less than ⁻1.

You can write ⁻5 < ⁻1 or ⁻1 > ⁻5.

Example 2

Order the numbers from least to greatest: ⁺6, ⁻3, ⁺9, ⁻8, ⁻1.

Locate the numbers on the number line.

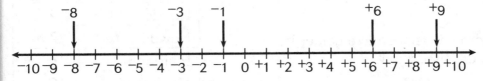

Since ⁻8 is the farthest to the left, it is the smallest number.
Since ⁺9 is the farthest to the right, it is the greatest number.

The numbers in order from least to greatest are:
⁻8, ⁻3, ⁻1, ⁺6, ⁺9

....

Compare using > or <.

1 ⁺6 ● ⁻4   **2** ⁻5 ● ⁻2   **3** ⁻8 ● ⁻7

4 ⁺21 ● ⁻9   **5** ⁺8 ● 0   **6** 0 ● ⁻1

7 ⁺2 ● ⁻6   **8** ⁻1 ● ⁻5   **9** ⁻9 ● 0

Positive and Negative Numbers (continued)

Fill in the missing numbers.

10 ⁻15, ⁻12, ⁻9, ■, ⁻3, ■

11 ⁺9, ⁺6, ■, 0, ■, ⁻6

12 ⁻4, ⁻8, ■, ⁻16, ■, ⁻24

13 0, ⁻2, ⁻4, ■, ■, ■

Compare using > or <.

14 ⁻2 ●, ⁻6

15 0 ● ⁻5

16 ⁻4 ● ⁺1

17 ⁻14°F ● ⁻25F

18 ⁻7°F ● ⁻1°F

19 ⁻5°F ● 0°F

The table at right shows the record low temperatures in five states. Use the table for Exercises 20–22.

State	Record Low Temperatures
Florida	⁻2
Hawaii	⁺7
Louisiana	⁻16
Mississippi	⁻19
Texas	⁻23

Source: Time Almanac 2000.

20 Is the record low temperature colder in Louisiana or Mississippi?

_____

21 Order the temperatures from lowest to highest.

_____

22 If the low temperature in Florida went down 4°F, what would be the new record low?

_____

23 **Test Prep** Choose the correct letter for each answer.

Which of the following numbers is greatest?

A ⁻2   **B** ⁻5   **C** ⁻7   **D** ⁻9   **E** NH

24 During a 30-minute period in January, the temperature rose 2°F from ⁻5°F. What was the new temperature?

F ⁻2°F   **G** ⁻3°F   **H** 2°F   **J** 3°F   **K** NH

Name _____

Positive and Negative Numbers

1 Which numbers complete the list?

$^-13, ^-12, ^-11, ^-10, ▓, ▓, ▓, ^-6, ^-5$

- **A** $^-8, ^-7, ^-6$
- **B** $^-9, ^-8, ^-7$
- **C** $^-10, ^-9, ^-8$
- **D** $^-11, ^-12, ^-13$

2 Which of the following is true?

- **F** $0 > 4$
- **H** $^-8 < ^-6$
- **G** $^-2 < ^-10$
- **J** $^-4 > 4$

3 Order the temperatures from least to greatest.

Temperatures (°C)				
Mon.	Tues.	Wed.	Thurs.	Fri.
+5	0	−1	−4	−2

- **A** $0, ^-1, ^-2, ^-4, 5$
- **B** $^-1, ^-2, ^-4, 0, 5$
- **C** $^-4, ^-2, ^-1, 0, 5$
- **D** $5, 0, ^-1, ^-2, ^-4$

4 Which symbol makes the sentence true?

$^-36 ● ^-28$

- **F** $>$
- **G** $=$
- **H** $<$
- **J** $+$

5

Which point is at $^-2$?

- **A** B
- **B** Z
- **C** W
- **D** P

6 Which of the following is true?

- **F** $^-39 < ^-63$
- **G** $^-21 > ^-17$
- **H** $0 < ^-5$
- **J** $^-14 > ^-19$

7 Which numbers are in order from least to greatest?

- **A** $^-2, ^-3, ^-9$
- **B** $^-2, ^-9, ^-3$
- **C** $^-9, ^-2, ^-3$
- **D** $^-9, ^-3, ^-2$

8 Which temperature is the coldest?

- **F** $^-1°F$
- **G** $0°F$
- **H** $^+6°F$
- **J** $^-5°F$

Oral Directions Choose the correct letter for each answer.

© Scott Foresman

23

Which two numbers would you add first when finding the sum of 34 + 98 + 66? Why? What is the sum of the three numbers?

Mental Math: Using Compatible Numbers and Compensation **LESSON PRACTICE**

Example 1

Find 13 + 21 + 37.

Look for compatible numbers. $13 + 21 + 37 = 50 + 21$

Add these numbers first. $= 71$

Example 2

Find 67 + 28.

Use compensation to adjust both numbers.

$$\begin{array}{r} 67 \\ + 28 \end{array}$$
Subtract 2 to adjust. → $$\begin{array}{r} 65 \\ + 30 \\ \hline 95 \end{array}$$
Add 2 to adjust.

Use mental math to find each sum or difference.

1 15 + 45 + 7 _____

2 38 + 16 + 12 _____

3 39 + 38 + 11 _____

4 58 + 9 + 22 _____

5 13 + 19 + 41 _____

6 7 + 23 + 8 _____

7 $\begin{array}{r} 54 \\ + 18 \\ \hline \end{array}$

8 $\begin{array}{r} 29 \\ + 24 \\ \hline \end{array}$

9 $\begin{array}{r} 43 \\ + 51 \\ \hline \end{array}$

10 $\begin{array}{r} 77 \\ - 38 \\ \hline \end{array}$

11 $\begin{array}{r} 53 \\ - 19 \\ \hline \end{array}$

12 $\begin{array}{r} 96 \\ - 89 \\ \hline \end{array}$

13 $\begin{array}{r} 33 \\ + 49 \\ \hline \end{array}$

14 $\begin{array}{r} 18 \\ + 36 \\ \hline \end{array}$

15 $\begin{array}{r} 49 \\ + 9 \\ \hline \end{array}$

16 $\begin{array}{r} 61 \\ - 43 \\ \hline \end{array}$

17 $\begin{array}{r} 92 \\ - 78 \\ \hline \end{array}$

18 $\begin{array}{r} 37 \\ - 29 \\ \hline \end{array}$

Mental Math: Using Compatible Numbers and Compensation (continued)

Use mental math to find each sum or difference.

19 $17 + 23 + 40$ _____

20 $46 + 18 + 14$ _____

21 $27 + 28 + 32$ _____

22
$$\begin{array}{r} 31 \\ + 53 \\ \hline \end{array}$$

23
$$\begin{array}{r} 74 \\ + 18 \\ \hline \end{array}$$

24
$$\begin{array}{r} 44 \\ + 37 \\ \hline \end{array}$$

25
$$\begin{array}{r} 36 \\ - 17 \\ \hline \end{array}$$

26
$$\begin{array}{r} 83 \\ - 65 \\ \hline \end{array}$$

27
$$\begin{array}{r} 76 \\ - 29 \\ \hline \end{array}$$

28 Kara read 23 books in September, 17 in October, and 31 in November. Use mental math to find how many books she read in all. _____

29 **Algebra** $41 + x + 19 = 83$. What does x equal? _____

30 Brad and Joe want to buy a new video game for $59. Brad has $26 and Joe has $14. How much more money do they need? _____

31 Billy earned $42 in week 1, $23 in week 2, $28 in week 3, and $38 in week 4. How much did he earn in the first three weeks? _____

32 **Test Prep** Choose the correct letter for each answer.

Chris has 23 compact disks, Bradley has 19, and Stephanie has 31. How many compact disks do they have in all?

A 50 **B** 82 **C** 73 **D** 70 **E** NH

33 $91 - 36 =$

F 45 **G** 55 **H** 47 **J** 90 **K** NH

Name _____

1 $1 + 63 + 19 =$

A 73   **D** 84

B 82   **E** NH

C 83

5 This week Marcus bought a CD player for $88 and a CD for $16. How much money did he spend?

A $94   **D** $114

B $104   **E** NH

C $106

2
$$\begin{array}{r} 46 \\ -\ 39 \\ \hline \end{array}$$

F 8   **J** 27

G 17   **K** NH

H 18

6
$$\begin{array}{r} 64 \\ -\ 18 \\ \hline \end{array}$$

F 42   **J** 56

G 44   **K** NH

H 46

3 Kayla scored 17 points, Melissa scored 23 points, and Tracy scored 15 points. How many points did they score in all?

A 40 points   **D** 55 points

B 45 points   **E** NH

C 50 points

7 Tamika had 95 beads. She used 47 of them on a school project. How many beads did she have left?

A 38 beads   **D** 142 beads

B 46 beads   **E** NH

C 47 beads

4 Carlos made 79 bookmarks. Tony made 53 bookmarks. How many more bookmarks did Carlos make?

F 26 bookmarks

G 27 bookmarks

H 36 bookmarks

J 132 bookmarks

K NH

8
$$\begin{array}{r} 36 \\ +\ 59 \\ \hline \end{array}$$

F 85   **J** 105

G 95   **K** NH

H 97

Oral Directions Use mental math to find each sum or difference in Exercises 1–8.

Which number is greater, 4,387,596 rounded to the nearest thousand or 4,387,596 rounded to the nearest hundred thousand? Explain.

Name _____

Rounding Numbers

Example 1

Round 79,485,360 to the nearest hundred thousand.

Step 1 Find the hundred thousands place.
79,<u>4</u>85,360

Step 2 Look at the digit to the right.
↓
79,4<u>8</u>5,360

Step 3 If the digit to the right is less than 5, round down. If the digit is 5 or greater, round up.

79,485,360 rounds to 79,500,000

Since 8 > 5, increase the hundred thousands place by 1.

Example 2

Round 341,71<u>8</u>,300 to the underlined place.

Step 1 The underlined digit is in the thousands place.
341,71<u>8</u>,300

Step 2 Look at the digit to the right.
↓
341,71<u>8</u>,300

Step 3 If the digit to the right is less than 5, round down. If the digit is 5 or greater, round up.

341,718,300 rounds to 341,718,000

Since 3 < 5, keep the thousands place the same.

Round each number to the nearest ten, hundred, thousand, ten thousand, and hundred thousand.

1 537,681

2 1,581,267

3 4,075,418

_____   _____   _____

_____   _____   _____

_____   _____   _____

_____   _____   _____

Rounding Numbers (continued)

Round each number to the nearest ten.

4 94,519 _____   **5** 3,194,764 _____

Round each number to the nearest hundred.

6 968,458 _____   **7** 1,265,906 _____

Round each number to the nearest thousand.

8 318,512 _____   **9** 26,906,294 _____

Round each number to the nearest ten thousand.

10 7,514,600 _____   **11** 82,437,894 _____

Round each number to the nearest hundred thousand.

12 21,561,300 _____   **13** 485,629,800 _____

Round each number to the underlined place.

14 12_5_,495   **15** 7,5_3_9,461   **16** 42,561,_7_35

_____   _____   _____

17 China has 124,212,400 children in primary school. To the nearest hundred thousand, how many children is this? _____

18 **Test Prep** Choose the correct letter for each answer.

Round 42,547,816 to the nearest ten thousand.

   A 42,540,000   **C** 42,500,000   **E** NH

   B 42,548,000   **D** 42,550,000

19 The earth is 12,756 kilometers in diameter across the equator. Round this number to the nearest hundred.

   F 12,700   **G** 12,800   **H** 12,760   **J** 13,000   **K** NH

Name _____

Rounding Numbers

1 A boat costs $8,699. Rounded to the nearest thousand dollars, how much did the boat cost?

A $8,000 D $9,000
B $8,600 E NH
C $8,700

2 The newspaper reported the attendance at the concert to be 364,918. What is the attendance rounded to the nearest ten thousand?

F 364,900 J 400,000
G 365,000 K NH
H 360,000

3 Which is 999,300,489 rounded to the nearest hundred?

A 999,300,000
B 999,300,400
C 999,300,490
D 1,000,000,000
E NH

4 Widget Mania, Inc., manufactured 2,487,200 trinkets last year. What is the number of trinkets they made rounded to the nearest hundred thousand?

F 2,500,000 J 2,000,000
G 2,490,000 K NH
H 2,400,000

5 Which is 25,314 rounded to the nearest ten thousand?

A 20,000 D 30,000
B 25,000 E NH
C 26,000

6 The 3-day sale at Rug World resulted in sales of $190,848. What is the sales rounded to the nearest thousand?

F $191,000 J $190,000
G $190,900 K NH
H $190,800

7 The company raised $17,517,859 for charity. Rounded to the nearest hundred thousand, how much money was raised?

A $17,000,000
B $17,500,000
C $17,500,900
D $18,000,000
E NH

8 Which is 163,219,299 rounded to the nearest ten?

F 163,220,000
G 163,219,300
H 163,219,290
J 160,000,000
K NH

Oral Directions Choose the correct letter for each answer.

© Scott Foresman

31

Name _____

Example 1

Use rounding to find an estimate.

287   +   439   +   168

rounds to   rounds to   rounds to

300   +   400   +   200   =   900

Example 2

Estimate 636 + 159 using front-end estimation.

Add the front digits in each number.   600 + 100 = 700

Adjust to account for the remaining digits.   36 + 59 is about 100.

636 + 159 is about 800.   700 + 100 = 800

Estimate each sum or difference by rounding.

1   57 + 81   **2**   493 + 125   **3**   583 − 308   **4**   4,684 + 2,073   **5**   1,327 − 958

Estimate each sum or difference by using front-end estimation.
Then adjust to find a closer estimate.

6   338 + 427   **7**   161 + 521   **8**   382 − 168   **9**   843 − 508   **10**   5,365 − 3,240

Estimate each sum using clustering.

11   62 + 59 + 58 + 61   **12**   18 + 21 + 20 + 19 + 22

_____   _____

Estimate each sum or difference by rounding.

13   39 + 52   **14**   218 + 393   **15**   967 − 315   **16**   6,118 + 2,729   **17**   3,040 − 997

Name _____

Estimation Strategies (continued)

Estimate each sum or difference by using front-end estimation.
Then adjust to find a closer estimate.

 359
+ 134

 226
+ 558

 629
− 443

 7,650
− 4,913

 8,312
+ 1,219

Estimate each sum using clustering.

 50 + 48 + 51

24 69 + 72 + 70 + 71

 33 + 36 + 35 + 34

_____   _____   _____

26 Morgan delivered 92 newspapers in January, 89 in
February, 88 in March, 90 in April, and 92 in May.
Estimate the total newspapers she delivered in the
first four months.   _____

27 **Algebra** Ivan wants a new bicycle that costs $129.
He has already saved $61. Estimate the additional
money he will need to save.
$61 + a = $129   Solve for a.   _____

28 **Math Reasoning** Shayla earns about $50 a week in tips. After six
weeks will she have enough money to buy a $429 television? Explain.

_____

_____

29 **Test Prep** Choose the correct letter for each answer.

What is the best estimate for $819 + $288?

A $1,000   **B** $1,200   **C** $900   **D** $1,100   **E** NH

30 Jerome scored 21 touchdowns in 1997, 19 in 1998, and 22 in 1999.
What is the best estimate for his touchdown in these three years?

F 60   **G** 50   **H** 65   **J** 70   **K** NH

Name _____

Estimation Strategies

1 Estimate 237 + 678 using rounding.

    A 600

    B 700

    C 800

    D 900

3 Estimate 36 + 40 + 42 using clustering.

    A 110

    B 120

    C 130

    D 140

2 Estimate 893 − 246 using front-end estimation. Then adjust.

    F 500

    G 550

    H 600

    J 650

4 Cory made $16, $14, $15, and $15 mowing lawns. Use clustering to estimate how much money Cory made mowing lawns.

    F $40   **H** $60

    G $50   **J** $70

Oral Directions Choose the correct letter for each answer.

Name _____

Estimation Strategies (continued)

5 Keesha scored an 89 her first game and a 73 her second game. Use rounding to estimate her total score.

A 160

B 170

C 180

D 190

6 Newell had 237 baseball cards in one box and 653 baseball cards in another. Use front-end estimation to estimate, then adjust, to find the total number of baseball cards Newell has.

F 800 cards

G 860 cards

H 890 cards

J 900 cards

7 Mr. Davis needs $7,800 to buy a used truck. He has $2,113. Use rounding to estimate the difference.

A $3,000

B $4,000

C $5,000

D $6,000

8 The airplane pilot recorded that the plane has traveled 591 miles on the trip so far. The total number of miles of the trip is 1,408. Estimate how many miles are left in the trip. Use rounding to the nearest hundred.

F 700 miles

G 800 miles

H 900 miles

J 1,000 miles

Ann paid $7.19 to mail a large package, $4.85 to mail a small package, and $0.37 to mail a letter. How much did she spend in all?

Adding Two- and Three-Digit Numbers

Example 1

Find 257 + 149.

Step 1 Add the ones. Regroup 16 ones as 1 ten and 6 ones.

```
   1
  257
+ 149
    6
```

Step 2 Add the tens. Regroup 10 tens as 1 ten and 0 ones.

```
  11
  257
+ 149
   06
```

Step 3 Add the hundreds.

```
  11
  257
+ 149
  406
```

Check by estimating: 300 + 100 = 400. The answer is reasonable because 406 is close to 400.

1
```
  36
+ 47
```

2
```
  53
+ 29
```

3
```
  175
+  48
```

4
```
$8.91
+ 2.26
```

5
```
  794
+ 138
```

6
```
  452
+ 398
```

7
```
$1.95
+ 0.99
```

8
```
  809
+  98
```

9
```
  257
+ 155
```

10
```
  642
+ 139
```

11
```
$0.78
  0.25
+ 0.34
```

12
```
  24
  18
+  5
```

13
```
  78
  63
+ 51
```

14
```
  139
   48
+  21
```

15
```
  514
  192
+ 237
```

Adding Two- and Three-Digit Numbers (continued)

16 75
       + 19

17 163
       + 47

18 421
       + 99

19 137
       + 168

20 $7.87
       + 0.95

21 $3.95
       + 1.88

22 596
       + 117

23 371
       + 259

24 448
       + 372

25 685
       + 96

26 51 + 18 + 6

27 652 + 81 + 27

28 149 + 450 + 13

29 Lauryssa read the menu at a restaurant and noticed that hamburgers cost $2.95 and chicken sandwiches cost $3.79. An order of fries costs $1.39. How much would a hamburger and an order of fries cost? _____

30 **Mental Math** Find 699 + 41. _____

31 **Mental Math** Find 809 + 61. _____

32 **Test Prep** Choose the correct letter for each answer.

Find 82 + 17 + 25.

A 124   **B** 104   **C** 122   **D** 114   **E** NH

33 Miguel spent $6.85 on a new book and $0.99 on a bookmark. How much did he spend?

F $7.74   **G** $8.75   **H** $7.84   **J** $6.84   **K** NH

Adding Two- and Three-Digit Numbers

ADDITIONAL PRACTICE

1 There are 28 days until Jan's birthday. Then there are 35 more days until her brother's birthday. How many days is it until Jan's brother's birthday?

A 7 days   **D** 63 days

B 35 days   **E** NH

C 53 days

2 Wyatt's Farm charges a fee for people to pick pumpkins in October. The fee is the same no matter how many pumpkins a person picks. The table shows how many pumpkins were picked in three days.

Pumpkins Picked	
Oct. 15	63
Oct. 16	212
Oct. 17	84

How many pumpkins were picked from Oct. 15 through Oct. 17?

F 259 pumpkins

G 349 pumpkins

H 359 pumpkins

J 379 pumpkins

K NH

3 817 + 129 =

A 688   **D** 947

B 938   **E** NH

C 946

4 The table shows the number of students in 3 elementary schools.

School	Number of Students
Oak Lane	273
Pine Street	326
Longfellow	315

How many students attend all 3 schools?

F 599 students

G 641 students

H 814 students

J 904 students

K NH

5 87 + 870 =

A 857   **D** 1,740

B 957   **E** NH

C 1,057

6 Erin paints and sells rocks to earn money. If she sold one rock for $1.29 and another for $3.22, how much did she earn?

F $5.51   **J** $1.93

G $4.51   **K** NH

H $4.41

Oral Directions Choose the correct letter for each answer.

© Scott Foresman

How much less does the lemonade cost than the juice?

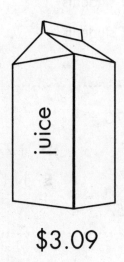

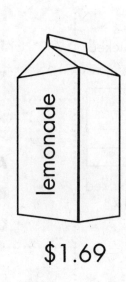

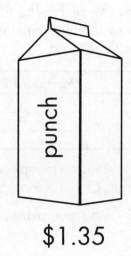

$3.09 $1.69 $1.35

Name _____

Subtracting Two- and Three-Digit Numbers

LESSON PRACTICE

Example

Find 823 − 265.

Step 1 Subtract the ones. Regroup 1 ten as 10 ones.

```
  1 13
 8 2̸ 3̸
− 2 6 5
─────────
       8
```

Step 2 Subtract the tens. Regroup 1 hundred as 10 tens.

```
 7 11 13
 8̸ 2̸ 3̸
−  2 6 5
─────────
    5 8
```

Step 3 Subtract the hundreds.

```
 7 11 13
 8̸ 2̸ 3̸
−  2 6 5
─────────
   5 5 8
```

Check by estimating: 800 − 300 = 500. The answer is reasonable because 558 is close to 500.

1.
```
  48
− 38
```

2.
```
  65
− 57
```

3.
```
  72
− 48
```

4.
```
 151
−  29
```

5.
```
 346
−  77
```

6.
```
 $0.92
+ 0.59
```

7.
```
 $9.12
− 5.65
```

8.
```
 768
−  79
```

9.
```
 411
− 162
```

10.
```
 214
− 156
```

11.
```
 $8.15
− 4.98
```

12.
```
 $7.50
− 0.91
```

13.
```
 640
− 289
```

14.
```
 512
−  96
```

15.
```
 435
− 157
```

16. 461 − 372

_____

17. 881 − 493

_____

18. 506 − 227

_____

© Scott Foresman

Name _____

Subtracting Two- and Three-Digit Numbers (continued)

19 76
− 49

20 65
− 28

21 175
− 86

22 251
− 94

23 $9.85
− 3.96

24 315
− 49

25 940
− 215

26 $8.05
− 1.57

27 712
− 393

28 631
− 452

29 560 − 373
_____

30 905 − 876
_____

31 413 − 299
_____

32 Students in the United States go to school for about 175 days each year, while students in China go to school for about 251 days. How many more days do Chinese students attend school?   _____

33 **Math Reasoning** Explain why the subtraction problem 81−16 requires regrouping.

_____

_____

_____

_____

34 **Test Prep** Choose the correct letter for each answer.

Find 641 − 283.

A 452   **B** 358   **C** 348   **D** 442   **E** NH

35 Robin had $9.15, but spent $5.89 of it on a new bracelet. How much money did she have left?

F $3.76   **G** $4.24   **H** $4.74   **J** $3.26   **K** NH

Subtracting Two- and Three-Digit Numbers ADDITIONAL PRACTICE

1
$$\begin{array}{r} 50 \\ -29 \\ \hline \end{array}$$

A 79   **D** 21

B 39   **E** NH

C 31

4 Of the 612 students at Jefferson School, 389 ride a bus to school. How many do not ride a bus?

F 223 students

G 277 students

H 323 students

J 377 students

K NH

2 The Green Street Hotel is adding a new wing to be completed in the year 2006. The new wing will hold more rooms. The table shows how the current number of rooms will compare with the number of rooms in 2006.

Rooms at Green St. Hotel	
Current	352
2006	430

How many rooms are being added?

F 782 rooms   **J** 78 rooms

G 182 rooms   **K** NH

H 122 rooms

5 The small yogurt has 218 grams. The large yogurt has 454 grams. How many more grams does the large yogurt have?

218 g   454 g

A 214 grams

B 218 grams

C 236 grams

D 672 grams

E NH

3 $8.12 − $2.90 =

A $11.02   **D** $4.82

B $6.22   **E** NH

C $5.22

6 734 − 87 =

F 643   **J** 821

G 648   **K** NH

H 753

Oral Directions Choose the correct letter for each answer.

A stadium has 248 luxury boxes and 900 bleacher seats. How many more bleacher seats are there than luxury boxes?

Subtracting Across Zeros

Example

Find 5,000 − 2,864.

There are no ones, tens, or hundreds. So these columns must be regrouped.

Step 1 Regroup 1 thousand as 10 hundreds.

Step 2 Regroup 1 hundred as 10 tens.

Step 3 Regroup 1 ten as 10 ones.

Step 4 Subtract.

Check by adding:

$$\begin{array}{r} 5,000 \\ -\ 2,864 \\ \hline 2,136 \end{array} \qquad \begin{array}{r} 2,136 \\ +\ 2,864 \\ \hline 5,000 \end{array}$$

You can also check by estimating: 5,000 − 3,000 = 2,000.
The answer is reasonable because 2,136 is close to 2,000.

1
$$\begin{array}{r} 300 \\ -\ 179 \\ \hline \end{array}$$

2
$$\begin{array}{r} 500 \\ -\ 483 \\ \hline \end{array}$$

3
$$\begin{array}{r} 9,000 \\ -\ 612 \\ \hline \end{array}$$

4
$$\begin{array}{r} 7,000 \\ -\ 1,294 \\ \hline \end{array}$$

5
$$\begin{array}{r} 3,000 \\ -\ 1,847 \\ \hline \end{array}$$

6
$$\begin{array}{r} 5,000 \\ -\ 4,105 \\ \hline \end{array}$$

7
$$\begin{array}{r} 6,000 \\ -\ 3,450 \\ \hline \end{array}$$

8
$$\begin{array}{r} 2,000 \\ -\ 999 \\ \hline \end{array}$$

9
$$\begin{array}{r} 1,000 \\ -\ 165 \\ \hline \end{array}$$

10
$$\begin{array}{r} 12,000 \\ -\ 5,514 \\ \hline \end{array}$$

11 40,008 − 6,193

12 8,000 − 2,140

13 5,000 − 3,451

Subtracting Across Zeros (continued)

14
900
− 465

15
200
− 146

16
1,000
− 843

17
5,030
− 1,945

18
9,400
− 3,895

19
6,000
− 4,163

20
2,000
− 1,406

21
8,000
− 5,473

22
30,000
− 20,721

23
70,000
− 43,563

24 3,050 − 2,173 _____

25 5,000 − 2,763 _____

26 10,000 − 8,916 _____

27 Jonna is reading a 300-page book. So far she has read 179 pages. How many pages does she have left to read? _____

28 A town with a population of 12,000 has 1,956 of its residents who regularly use 3 exercise facilities. How many residents do not use an exercise facility? _____

29 **Mental Math** Find 10,000 − 9,999. _____

30 **Test Prep** Choose the correct letter for each answer.

Find 6,000 − 3,578.

A 3,578   **B** 2,578   **C** 3,422   **D** 2,422   **E** NH

31 A basketball arena has 5,000 seats. If a crowd of 4,135 people attends a game, how many seats are empty?

F 1,135   **G** 865   **H** 135   **J** 1,865   **K** NH

Subtracting Across Zeros

1 3,000 − 1,095 =

A 1,905   **D** 4,095

B 2,005   **E** NH

C 2,095

5 87,004 − 25,987 =

A 60,017   **D** 112,991

B 61,017   **E** NH

C 62,983

2 Felicia planted 135 bulbs in her garden. She began with 300 bulbs in all to plant. How many more bulbs does she still need to plant?

F 155 bulbs   **J** 435 bulbs

G 165 bulbs   **K** NH

H 175 bulbs

6 Mr. Flores must survey 5,000 people about their favorite fast-food choices. He has already surveyed 2,683 people. How many more people must he survey?

F 2,316   **J** 3,317

G 2,317   **K** NH

H 2,427

3 84,909 − 24,199 =

A 60,710

B 60,890

C 109,108

D 109,998

E NH

7 Max bought a new computer game for $17.85. He paid with a $20.00 bill. If the price included tax, how much change should Max receive?

A $3.25   **D** $2.10

B $3.15   **E** NH

C $2.25

4 Terry bought a notebook for $3.28. He gave the clerk $10.00. How much change should he get back?

F $6.82   **J** $6.12

G $6.72   **K** NH

H $6.21

8
$$4,000$$
$$- 2,981$$

F 2,981   **J** 1,019

G 1,981   **K** NH

H 1,129

Oral Directions Choose the correct letter for each answer.

The population of Danesville is 43,602 and the population of Minton is 38,986. How many more people live in Danesville than in Minton?

Name _____

Adding and Subtracting Greater Whole Numbers LESSON PRACTICE

Example 1

Find 15,608 + 12,573.

```
    1 1
  15,608
+ 12,573
  ──────
  28,181
```

Step 1 Add the ones. Regroup if you can.
Step 2 Add the tens. Regroup if you can.
Step 3 Add the hundreds. Regroup if you can.
Step 4 Continue to add.

Example 2

Find 3,810 − 1,907.

```
  2 18 0 10
  3,8̶1̶0̶
− 1,907
  ──────
  1,903
```

Step 1 Subtract the ones. Decide if you need to regroup.
Step 2 Subtract the tens. Decide if you need to regroup.
Step 3 Subtract the hundreds. Decide if you need to regroup.
Step 4 Subtract the thousands.

1
```
  53,648
+  8,052
```

2
```
   1,693
+ 18,024
```

3
```
  37,960
− 15,838
```

4
```
  76,612
+  8,908
```

5
```
     377
+  4,804
```

6
```
  6,980
−   972
```

7 4,338 + 1,615 + 307

_____

8 17,612 − 8,032

_____

© Scott Foresman

49

Adding and Subtracting Greater Whole Numbers (continued)

9 $64,319
+ 3,680

10 3,946
+ 1,073

11 6,261
− 1,334

12 $4,364
− 1,805

13 683
1,270
+ 3,308

14 38,042
− 8,532

15 15,410
− 6,553

16 $6,384
+ 4,628

17 581 + 379 + 656

_____

18 73,450 − 5,117

_____

19 19,562 − 8,743

_____

Use the table at the right for Exercises 20–23.

Annual Wages	
Maria	$47,387
Jeremy	$28,405
Max	$36,975
Julie	$27,832
Chan	$15,083
Nicole	$41,670

20 Max and Nicole are married. What are their total annual wages? _____

21 **Algebra** Maria wants to make $50,000. How much of a raise does she need to make $50,000? $47,387 + n = $50,000   Solve for n.

_____

22 **Mental Math** Julie is getting a $3,000 raise in her annual wages. What will be her annual wages? Will she make more than her husband, Jeremy? _____

23 Chan works part time. Next year he will begin working full time and get his wages doubled. What will be his new annual wages? _____

24 **Test Prep** Choose the correct letter for each answer.

396 + 4,114 + 5,876

A 10,376   **B** 10,386   **C** 10,286   **D** 9,990   **E** NH

25 Find the value of x + y if x = $5,614 and y = $9,018.

F $4,632   **G** $14,622   **H** $15,632   **J** $14,632   **K** NH

Name _____

1
   72,189
 + 23,556

   A 96,635   **D** 45,633
   B 95,745   **E** NH
   C 95,635

2 William scores 79,890 points on a computer game. Sarah scores 58,009 points. How many more points did William score than Sarah?

   F 21,881 points
   G 21,891 points
   H 21,899 points
   J 137,899 points
   K NH

3 36,042 + 7,898 =

   A 33,940   **D** 43,940
   B 43,830   **E** NH
   C 43,930

4 Juan and Chris are partners. What is their total score?

   F 66,033
   G 58,878
   H 37,976
   J 37,958
   K NH

Score Sheet	
Game	**Score**
Sean	35,908
Chris	22,970
Juan	14,988
Tamika	43,063
Yo	12,309

5
   62,005
 − 11,003

   A 51,002
   B 51,008
   C 53,002
   D 71,002
   E NH

6 4,445 + 821 + 5,966 =

   F 10,411   **J** 11,332
   G 11,132   **K** NH
   H 11,232

7 74,239 − 14,855 =

   A 89,094   **D** 59,384
   B 60,624   **E** NH
   C 59,624

8 Jermaine has 45,334 points on a computer game. Tyler has 5,899 points. How many more points does Jermaine have?

   F 39,335   **J** 40,565
   G 39,435   **K** NH
   H 40,465

Oral Directions Choose the correct letter for each answer.

Tools Contents

Name _____

Tool 1

Place-Value Charts

ONES

hundreds | tens | ones

THOUSANDS | ONES

hundred thousands | ten thousands | thousands | hundreds | tens | ones

MILLIONS | THOUSANDS | ONES

hundred millions | ten millions | millions | hundred thousands | ten thousands | thousands | hundreds | tens | ones

© Scott Foresman

53

Name _____

Base-Ten Blocks, Set 1

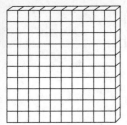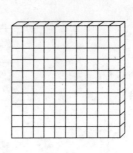

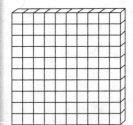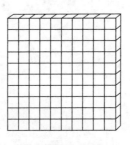

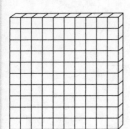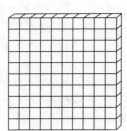

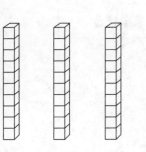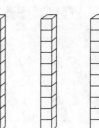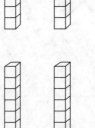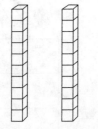

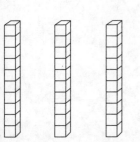

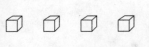

Word Web

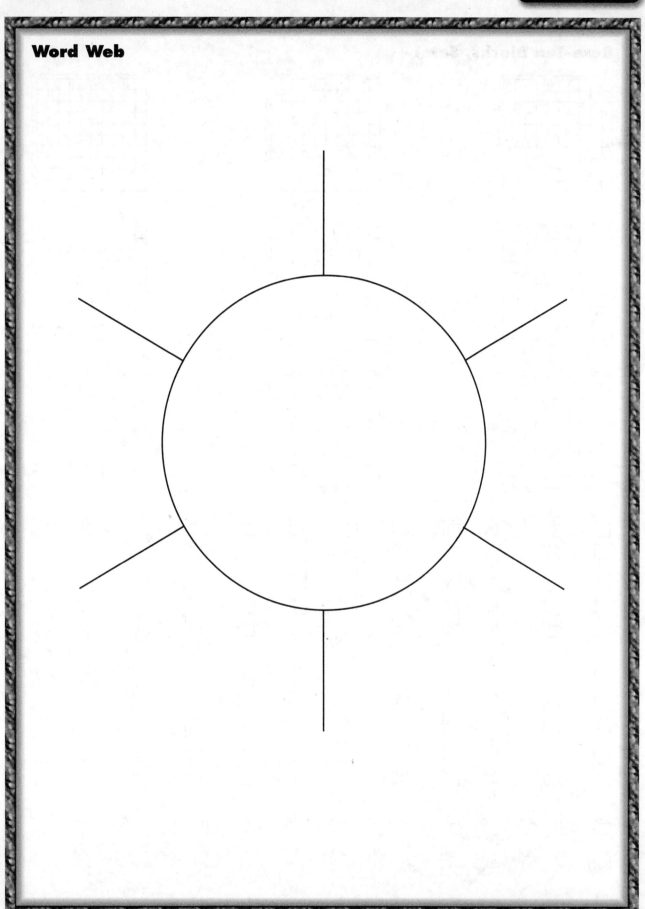

Name _____

Base-Ten Blocks, Set 1

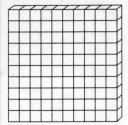
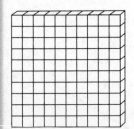
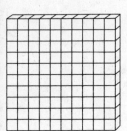
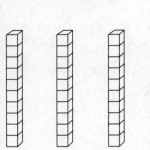
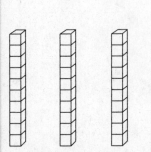

Name _____

Base-Ten Blocks, Set 1

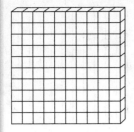
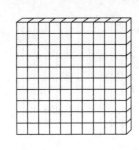
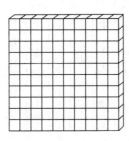
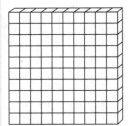
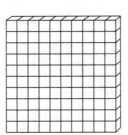
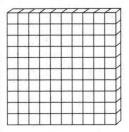
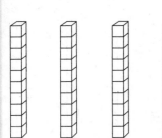
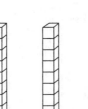
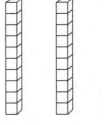

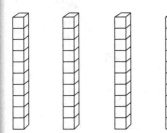
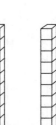
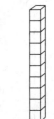
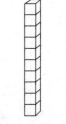

Name _____

Tool 6

Base-Ten Blocks, Set 1

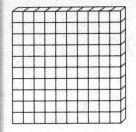 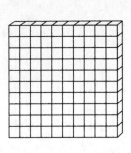 (blocks)

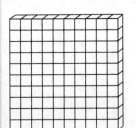 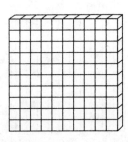

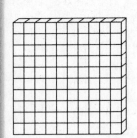 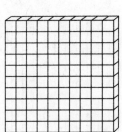

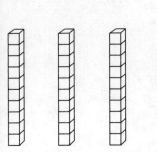 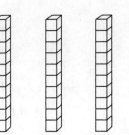

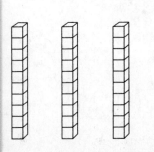 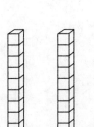  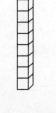

Base-Ten Blocks, Set 2